LET'S VISIT...

NORTHERN IRELAND

Annabelle Lynch

W
FRANKLIN WATTS
LONDON·SYDNEY

First published in 2015 by
Franklin Watts
338 Euston Road
London NW1 3BH

Franklin Watts Australia
Level 17/207 Kent Street
Sydney NSW 2000

© 2015 Franklin Watts

HB ISBN 978 1 4451 3707 0
Library eBook ISBN: 978 1 4451 3708 7

Dewey classification number: 941.6

Editor: Julia Bird
Designer: Jeni Child

Printed in China

Photo acknowledgements: Ian Barnes/Shutterstock: 4bl. Roger Bradley/istockphoto: 6b. catwalker/Shutterstock: 14. De Luan/Alamy: 1, 4-5. tamsin dove/Shutterstock: front cover, 3bl, 8t, 20. Stephen Emerson/Alamy: 9c. Christopher Hill/Scenic Ireland/Alamy: 21b. iBlueman/istockphoto: 8b. Isifa Image Service sro/Alamy: 7b. Sergey Korotkov/Dreamstime: 7c. Paul Lindsay/Alamy: 18t. David Lyons/Alamy: 10. Peter Mahley/Alamy: 15tr, 15b. Adrian Mcglynn/Dreamstime: 17b. Jane McIlroy/Shutterstock: 11b. Kirsty McLaren/Alamy: 12, 16b. B O'Kane/Alamy: 17c. Paetzhh/Dreamstime: 13t. D Primrose/Alamy: 19c. Radharc Images/Alamy: 3br, 7t, 11t, 17t. rdniblock/istockphoto: 13c. Trondur/Dreamstime: 21t. Vanderwolf Images/Shutterstock: 2, 15tl. Serg Zastavkin/Shutterstock: 5tr. Razvan Zinica/Shutterstock: 18b

Every attempt has been made to clear copyright. Should there be any inadvertent omission, please apply to the Publishers for rectification.

Franklin Watts is a division of Hachette Children's Books, an Hachette UK company.
www.hachette.co.uk

CONTENTS

Words in **bold** are in the glossary.

LET'S VISIT
NORTHERN
IRELAND

Northern Ireland is on the island of Ireland. It shares a land **border** with the Republic of Ireland in the south and west. The rest of Northern Ireland is surrounded by sea.

What does it look like?

The Northern Ireland countryside is green and hilly. There are bigger mountains in the Mourne and Sperrin **ranges**. Northern Ireland has a long, beautiful coastline, with rocky islands dotted around it.

Northern Ireland has lots of long, beautiful beaches like White Park Bay.

A busy shopping street in the heart of Belfast. →

Round, rolling hills known as drumlins can be found across Northern Ireland.

Cities

Belfast is the **capital** city of Northern Ireland. It is also the biggest city. Northern Ireland is divided into six **counties**. Belfast is found in both County Antrim and County Down.

When to go

Northern Ireland has warm summers and cool winters. It can rain at any time of year, but the spring or summer months are usually the best time to visit.

TRAVEL TIP

People from Northern Ireland often call Northern Ireland 'Ulster'.

RATHLIN ISLAND

Rugged Rathlin Island lies off the coast of Northern Ireland. It is just ten kilometres from one end of the island to the other.

Island home

Rathlin is the only **inhabited** island in Northern Ireland. Around 100 people live here all year round. The tiny primary school has just nine pupils!

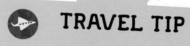

TRAVEL TIP

On a clear day you can see as far away as Scotland's Mull of Kintyre.

Rathlin's East Lighthouse has been warning ships of danger since 1856.

Getting there

Getting to Rathlin Island is an adventure! You can take a ferry there from Ballycastle harbour if the weather is good. It takes around 30 splashy minutes.

Ferries sail to Rathlin Island from Ballycastle up to ten times a day.

Bird haven

Rathlin Island is famous for its sea birds. Make sure you visit the RSPB centre to see thousands of puffins, guillemots and peregrine falcons. On the way, you might see some seals sunning themselves on a rock!

Puffins can be seen in spring and early summer.

A huge colony of guillemots on Rathlin Island.

OTHER **ISLANDS** TO VISIT:

Devenish Island

White Island

Coney Island

DUNLUCE CASTLE

Dunluce Castle in County Antrim is perched on the edge of a sheer cliff, giving it spectacular views over the surrounding sea.

Castle collapse!

There has been a castle at Dunluce since the 14th century. According to **legend**, the MacDonnell family lived there until 1639 when part of the castle, including the kitchens, fell into the sea one stormy night! Since then the castle has been empty, apart from visitors.

Many parts of the castle have been standing for hundreds of years.

TRAVEL TIP

Make sure you visit the Mermaid's Cave hidden away below the castle.

 Dunluce Castle is one of Northern Ireland's most famous sights.

Exploring

Today, the castle is mostly in **ruins**, but it is still well worth a visit. You have to cross a narrow bridge to get to the castle itself. Once inside, you can explore the castle's rooms and towers by yourself or go on a guided tour to discover more about the castle's history.

OTHER **CASTLES** TO SEE:

Carrickfergus

Dunseverick

Enniskillen

BALLYCASTLE

If you like going to the beach, Ballycastle is one of the best beaches in Northern Ireland.

Sunny sands

Ballycastle beach stretches for a kilometre along the coast of County Antrim. It has fine, golden sand and is surrounded by high, grassy **dunes**.

Ballycastle beach on a sunny day. The cliffs of nearby Fair Head can be seen in the distance.

In the water

You can paddle, swim or even surf in the rolling waves off Ballycastle beach. Take care as there are no lifeguards on duty. Make sure an adult is always with you.

Time to fish

Ballycastle Is a great place to go fishing as there are plenty of fish to catch. You can cast your line from rocks at the end of the beach or join a fishing tour which will take you out to sea.

You can catch fish such as cod, pollock and mackerel off Ballycastle beach.

TRAVEL TIP

The nearby town of Ballycastle has a festival called Lammas in August. There are stalls, music and lots of **traditional** food on offer, including 'Yellow Man', a type of honeycomb.

OTHER GREAT
BEACHES
TO VISIT:

Portstewart Strand
Downhill Beach
Benone Strand

11

BELFAST ZOO

Meet the animals at Belfast Zoo! This great zoo opened in 1934 and is one of Northern Ireland's top attractions.

Animal home

The zoo is home to over 150 different **species** of animal, from lions, tigers and elephants to apes, anteaters and warty pigs! Many of the animals are at risk where they live in the wild.

 Seals bask in the sun at Belfast Zoo.

Walk about

It is a good idea to follow one of the planned walks to see as many animals as possible. You can do a big cat walk, monkey walk or penguin and sealion walk, among others.

Make sure you meet the meerkats on a walk around the zoo.

Warm and wild

If it is rainy or cold outside, make sure you visit the Rainforest House. The plants and animals there have been chosen to make it feel just like a tropical **rainforest** and the temperature is always a warm 27°C!

TRAVEL TIP

Look out for animal feeding times to see hungry animals in action!

OTHER GREAT ANIMAL PARKS:

Exploris Aquarium

The Ark Open Farm

Seaforde Tropical Butterfly House

13

TITANIC BELFAST

Visit Titanic Belfast to learn the story of the famous ship *Titanic*, which sank in the Atlantic Ocean over a hundred years ago.

The voyage

The *Titanic* was built in a Belfast **shipyard**. It set sail on its first voyage to New York on 10 April 1912, but just four days later it hit an **iceberg** and sank within hours. Over 1,500 passengers died in the icy seas.

OTHER GREAT
PLACES
TO VISIT NEARBY:

Ulster Museum
Botanic Gardens
Carrickfergus Castle

The *Titanic* was the biggest ship in the world at the time. It could carry over 2,000 passengers.

 The Titanic Belfast building is even the same height as the *Titanic*.

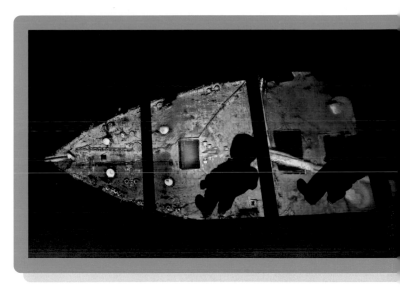

The building

Titanic Belfast opened in April 2012, exactly 100 years after the famous ship was **launched**. It is located just 100 metres from where the *Titanic* was built, and even looks like the front of a ship.

 This spooky special effect shows the wreck of the *Titanic* sitting on the seabed.

See for yourself

 Titanic Belfast has nine **galleries**, each bringing the *Titanic*'s story to life with photos, **artefacts**, videos and special effects. You can watch as the ship is launched, shiver as it sinks beneath the waves and even explore its wreck at the bottom of the Atlantic.

TRAVEL TIP

In the Fitting Out gallery you can visit a **replica** ship cabin and see the menu for the last lunch served on the *Titanic*.

ULSTER MUSEUM

If you are interested in finding out about the world around you, make sure you visit Ulster Museum in Belfast.

Treasures old and new

Ulster Museum is full of amazing things to discover from Northern Ireland and around the world. You can find out about the **shipwreck** treasures found at the bottom of the sea off the Irish coast, see the only dinosaur bones discovered in Ireland, and learn about the first people to settle here over 9,000 years ago. You can also see an Ancient Egyptian **mummy**, learn all about space rocks and shiver at a gruesome giant squid!

A natural history gallery at Ulster Museum.

Get up close with an Edmontosaurus dinosaur **skeleton**!

Discover and do

The museum's three discovery centres really bring the museum to life. In Discover Art you can make your own amazing pieces of art and solve giant puzzles and games. In Discover Nature you can handle fossils, see a real dinosaur's egg and look at butterflies and bugs under a **microscope**. In Discover History you can build pots, dress up in old costumes and have a go at being an **archaeologist** for the day!

These gold and silver coins were found in the wreck of the Spanish ship *La Girona*, which sank in the sea off Northern Ireland in 1588.

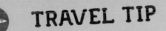

TRAVEL TIP

If it's sunny, have a picnic lunch outside the museum in the surrounding Botanic Gardens.

OTHER GREAT **MUSEUMS** TO EXPLORE:
Ulster Folk and Transport Museum
Armagh Planetarium
Crumlin Road Gaol

17

LUUGH NEACH

Lough Neagh is an enormous lake found in the heart of Northern Ireland. It supplies Northern Ireland with almost half of its drinking water.

 ## The lake

Lough Neagh is one of the biggest lakes in Europe, stretching nearly 30 kilometres long and 10 kilometres wide. It is a haven for all kinds of wildlife, especially birds, and a very popular place to visit.

 You might see Whooper swans like these on a visit to Lough Neagh.

↓ Lough Neagh on a sunny afternoon.

On the water

There is lots to do on the lake itself. You can go on a boat trip to visit the Lough's two islands – Ram's Island and Coney Island – or just explore the lake for yourself on the canoe trail.

↑ Get on your bike to explore the beautiful countryside around Lough Neagh.

PLACES **TO VISIT** NEARBY:

Tannaghmore Gardens

World of Owls

Portmore Lough Nature Reserve

Around and about

The lake is surrounded by woods and meadows and dotted with little beaches. A 180-kilometre cycle trail leads around the lake and is a great way to enjoy the views – though you might not make it all the way around!

TRAVEL TIP

If you want to stay at the lake for a night or two, pitch a tent at one of the lake's camping sites.

THE GIANT'S CAUSEWAY

The Giant's Causeway is made up of around 40,000 columns of rock.

The Giant's Causeway is Northern Ireland's top tourist attraction and one of the most famous places in the world.

Rocky place

The Giant's Causeway was formed millions of years ago when **volcanic eruptions** made hot rock called lava spill out across the coastline. When it cooled, the rock formed shapes called columns. Some had six sides, others had seven or eight. The columns fitted together to make amazing patterns.

 ## See for yourself

Today, you can explore the wonders of the Giant's Causeway for yourself. There are walking trails all around the area, or you can join a guided tour. Look out for some remarkable rock shapes along the way, such as the Giant's Boot and Organ Pipes (left).

The gigantic Organ Pipes stretch 12 metres into the sky.

Find out more

Make sure you go to the Tourist Information Centre during your visit. You can learn about how the Giant's Causeway was formed and hear all the legends about this famous place, including the story of the giant Finn McCool who gave the causeway its name.

TRAVEL TIP

It is amazing to watch the sunset over the Giant's Causeway.

Make sure you stop for a break at the Tourist Centre.

OTHER **GREAT PLACES** TO GO NEARBY:

Carrick-a-Rede Rope Bridge

Mount Stewart House & Gardens

Dunseverick Castle

MAP OF NORTHERN IRELAND

N

SPERRIN MOUNTAINS

BELFAST

MOURNE

KEY:

1 Rathlin Island
2 Dunluce Castle
3 Ballycastle
4 Belfast Zoo

5 Titanic Belfast
6 Ulster Museum
7 Lough Neagh
8 Giant's Causeway

GLOSSARY

archaeologist
Someone who digs up objects to find out about the past

artefact
An object, such as a piece of jewellery, that has been made by people

border
A line that divides two countries

capital
The city where a country's government meets

colony
A group of animals living together in a place

county
An area in a country that has its own local government

dunes
Big hills made of sand

gallery
A room in a museum that has lots of interesting things to look at

iceberg
A huge piece of ice that floats in the sea

inhabited
Lived in

launch
To send out to sea

legend
An old story

microscope
An instrument you can use to make things look bigger

mummy
A person's body that has been specially treated and wrapped in bandages

range
A group of mountains

replica
A copy of something

rainforest
Thick forest where there is a lot of rain

ruins
The parts of a building that are still standing when the rest of it has fallen down

shipwreck
When a ship breaks apart at sea

shipyard
A place where ships are built

skeleton
All the bones in a body joined together

species
A group of animals, such as dogs, that share many things in common and can breed together

traditional
Things such as food, clothes or music that have been the same for a long time

volcanic eruption
When hot rocks and ashes are thrown out of a volcano

INDEX

FURTHER INFORMATION

Books

Fact Cat: Northern Ireland by Alice Harman (Wayland, 2014)

Living in the UK: Northern Ireland by Annabelle Lynch (Franklin Watts, 2014)

Websites

www.discovernorthernireland.com

www.nmni.com/um/Visiting-Information/ Discovery-Zones-for-kids

www.titanicbelfast.com

Every effort has been made by the Publishers to ensure that the websites are suitable for children, and that they contain no inappropriate or offensive material. However, because of the nature of the Internet, it is impossible to guarantee that the contents of these sites will not be altered. We strongly advise that Internet access is supervised by a responsible adult.